The Watch by the Sea

Richard Brown

Illustrated by Annabel Large

CAMBRIDGE
UNIVERSITY PRESS

When I was younger and lived by the sea in New Zealand,
my mother gave me a watch. It was small, gold and precious.
It was my first watch, and it glittered on my wrist like a jewel.

I used to wind my watch each night, and I felt comforted by its tiny tick.

I used to spend long, hot days playing by the rock-pools with my older brother and sister. We chased cocklebullies in the still waters. These were like little snails without shells, and they could wriggle away from our fingers at great speed.

I loved to paddle in the rock-pools, or just lie on the shore
and watch the waves curl and fall with the light in them.

My mother told me not to wear my new watch on the beach, in case it got wet. But sometimes I couldn't resist taking it out with me. I tried hard not to get it wet.

When I wanted to go into the waves, or when I wanted to
plunge my arms deep into the rock-pools, I'd take off my
watch. I'd place it on the wooden landing-stage that jutted out
into the sea.

One day, I left my gold watch on the landing-stage. I paddled nearby in the waves.

Then my brother called to me, and I ran off to play with him. I forgot all about my watch.

When Mum called us in for tea, I left my watch behind.

Now, when I think about my watch, I can see it reflecting the last of the sun's rays. I can see a gull gliding above it. I imagine my watch growing dark until the pale moon crept over it.

It was only when I climbed into bed and tried to take my watch off, that I remembered where I'd left it. I couldn't believe I'd forgotten it.

I pretended to myself that I'd left it in the bathroom, or that it had slipped down under the bed.

I searched, hoping that I would find it. But of course, I didn't. What was I to do?

I lay in my bed. I was filled with a sort of slow panic.
I imagined my mother's sighs, my father's frowns, my sister's
teasing, my brother's gleeful laugh.

My precious watch, a gift from my mother – lost!
In the darkness my face grew hot with guilt.

Everyone in the house was asleep. I eased myself out of bed and placed my bare feet carefully on the floor. I pushed up the window and I slipped one leg over the sill.

A cool breeze curled around me. I paused.

My heart beat wildly. I was afraid of the night. I was afraid of the moonlit shadows and of the sound of the distant waves splashing on the beach.

My feet picked their way down the pebble path.
The gate creaked loudly. I froze with fear. I stared at
the house, expecting lights to blaze in the windows.

What would my family say if they saw me standing there in
my nightie? It was past midnight – how angry they would be.
I wanted to run back and bury myself in my warm bed.

But I turned towards the sea.

The waves purred in the moonlight. I picked my way
carefully over pebbles and shells and rock-pools. My feet were
used to this rough shore. But the beach looked different by
moonlight. It looked like another planet, and I felt that I was
the only person on it.

I kept my eyes fixed on the dark shadow of the landing-stage.
I was too afraid to look left or right.

Would my watch still be there?

Then I stopped.

Something seemed different. The waves were louder,
closer and bigger.

Suddenly, I had reached the landing-stage. I knocked my shins against it, and bent to steady myself. Then I knew. My heart lurched.

The tide had crept in. The tide had slipped its cold, white fingers around my watch, and taken it to the bottom of the sea.

I think I let out a cry. Then I turned, with panic
rising inside me.

How alone I felt on that dark beach. What if the tide
suddenly surged and snatched me too?

I fled. It seemed as if all the shadows of the night were
chasing me. The waves deafened me.

I rushed over the beach and crashed through the garden
gate. I scrambled through the open window.

I was safe again. But my watch had gone.

I shivered in my cool bed. I could not change the fact that
I had lost my watch. I wished so hard for it to be there,
ticking quietly by my bedside. I wished that I had remembered
my watch.

I imagined myself running down the beach, and snatching my watch from the waves just in time.

I dreaded the morning.

When I fell asleep I dreamt of my watch ticking
at the bottom of the sea.

In the morning, I stared at my bare wrist. My heart felt bare too. I dared not tell my mother, or the rest of my family, that I had lost my watch.

I put on a long-sleeved blouse to cover the white patch on my wrist.

For years, I told no-one about the lost watch and about
the midnight hunt. But the memory of it has ticked on
all this time.